It was a hot day.

Billy and Tom went to play in the pond.

Milly and Tilly went to look for Billy and Tom.

They went to look for Billy and Tom in the trees.

No Billy! No Tom!

They went to look for Billy and Tom in the bushes.

No Billy! No Tom!

They went to look for Billy and Tom in the hut.

No Billy!   No Tom!

They went to look for Billy and Tom in the pond.

Yes! Billy was in the pond.

Yes! Tom was in the pond.

All the little pigs went into the hut to look for mum and dad.

Mum was happy to see the little pigs.

Dad was happy to see the little pigs.